A BROOM TO FLY

For you and me,
our children,
and those who come after.

–A Unique Angle On EXPECTATIONS!

Jumping over the broom is an ancient African matrimonial custom. Since marriage is the only association that exercises a person in every facet of expectations, I have applied the motif of two people jumping over the broom, in this book. However, the theme: **A Broom To Fly** applies to any situation in which an expectation may become a great expectation, and the sky the limit.

The focus of the book is the uplifting nature of the private, self-management talks you have with yourself.

Glenwood

A BROOM TO FLY

SELF-MANAGEMENT TALKS

Written & Illustrated
by
GLENWOOD LAWRENCE

Growth Publishers, Inc. ● New York

Library Of Congress Catalog Card Number: 90-82823

ISBN 0-9624719-4-1

Printed in the United States of America

CONTENTS

Love as An Emotion 11

Personal Matters....................................... 37

Saying it,
and doing it 57

Choices... 77

An Inside Job 91

Deja vu 107

PREFACE

Desire has generated expectations of
TOTAL HAPPINESS
through a friendship
or the anticipated results of a project.

Values are assigned...
the expectation becomes a great expectation.
Hands tremble for fear the light
will go out —
*and trembling hands **make** the light go out.*

...In the dark
voices holler:
"How can one's love be sin?"

Love, then, is seen as a culprit...

iii

The Author

Glenwood Lawrence, born in Kingston, Jamaica, West Indies, is an artist with 27 one-man exhibitions of paintings and drawings to his credit, as well as participation in many group exhibitions and graphic arts projects. Besides the series: *Self-Management Talks With Yourself*, which also includes *My God!*, the sequel to this book, Lawrence has written and illustrated the art book: *Railways of Jamaica* (Kingston Publishers Ltd.), and the novel: *Exodus 500*. He also illustrated *Nanny Town*, the novel by V.S. Reid (Jamaica Publishing Company).

Lawrence is also an accomplished musician and recording artiste. To his credit: *The Great Debate*, *Enter His Presence With Praise* (singles) and *Searching For Dad* (album).

STATEMENT: *"I listen quietly to the love in the hearts of the people around me; their love for life, their need to understand and to be understood, their desire to appreciate and to be appreciated, and I hear, and see, and feel, in all of that... myself. Expressing this love is the rhythm of my existence. And in everything that I do, I seek ways of expressing this love -- fresh, interesting ways of saying: "I Love You...""*

ACKNOWLEDGMENTS

I thank God, the Source of inspiration, for the many people and circumstances that have heightened my perception. The list of acknowledgments would far exceed the text if I were to name everyone whose kindness in some way contributed to the reality of this book. There are people who have helped by just being there (like my parents). Others have worked directly on the project... like the fiery proofreader Dina Levine, and editor Susan Hoover. And there are people who have done both. Thanks to my wife, Delores and children: Shawnette and Andrea, who worked with me while I made odysseys into timelessness.

A note of appreciation to: Rev. Sam Stewart of Kingston Jamaica, who, in the early stages, told me, "Do not lose faith, and do not tire of well-doing"; Bishop James F. Copeland, ("God's Cop") of New York, whose kindness and vision are like great pillars to the international church community; to the memory of the late author James Baldwin (U-Mass), who said this book would one day speak to a lot of people; to professors Michael Thelwell, Andrew Salkey, (U-Mass); Prof. Mervyn Morris (UWI, Kingston) who took the mickey out of a fledgling writer... Dr. Marceline Watler, Chris Blackwell, Marianne Faithfull, Cliff Gardner (Author, Screenwriter); Augie and Pat Mellone, Brooklyn; Ron Antonio of *Critical Edge*; the staff of Graphic Dimensions Press, Brooklyn; to Mike Henry of Kingston Publishers Ltd.; and to the memory of the late Jamaican Author Victor Stafford Reid.

My thanks also goes to fellow-members of the following organizations, through which I've been able to combine perceptions of Art, Music and Literature into one body: *Association of Caribbean American Artists, Inc.; American Society of Authors, Composers and Publishers; American Federation of Musicians; South Florida Screen Writers Guild, Inc. and the Caribbean American Chamber of Commerce and Industry, Inc...*

Ahem!

See what I mean..? So, to all the people who have, in some way, helped me to keep both feet on the ground.. **Thank You!**

My little children, let us love
not in words neither in tongues;
but in deed and in truth.
1 John 3:18

CHAPTER ONE

LOVE AS AN EMOTION

LOVE
AS AN EMOTION

This chapter features
talks for adjusting expectations.

Do you ask because
you really care,
or simply because
you want to
say something?

I care as much
as you're upset.
Now, what's
your situation?

An expectation grew into
a great expectation . . .

. . . and the sky
became the limit . . .

However . . .

Split . . .

Tried to patch
up . . .

But . . .

That's the
situation.

And there are
other things
I can't even
talk about!

21

I am Conscience.
Have you prepared your mind to find answers,
or are you simply mad?
Who are you, anyway?

Prepared
my mind?
I'm really mad!

Why do friends
part?
That's one of my
questions!
Why, really, do friends part?

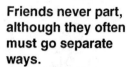

Friends never part,
although they often
must go separate
ways.

Friends never part?
So
what do you
call
a split?

24

I see love as an emotion
that too often causes wrath,
when inspiring PEACE and
HAPPINESS
is what it really should do.

**Would you have felt better
if your companion
had done everything
you wished,
without hesitation
or question?**

Well . . .
who wouldn't?

Would you have done
everything your companion
desired without hesitation
or question?
Be honest
with yourself.

You're implying:
"do unto others
as you would
have them
do unto you..."

**Maybe you
should give
that a try.**

**As a matter
of fact,
your chances
of being hurt
would be
less.**

**There comes a
time to search
our feelings
inside out,
to come to know
what the pains
of love are
all about,
and what makes
them real.**

Hmmmmmm...

I must
see her!

Let's make
our relationship
work positively.

Can you respect
the fact that
I am an individual
with my own
values?

Well,
I've done a much
better job on my
expectations than before.
I'm not perfect,
but I'm learning,
and so are you.
Besides, I'm
wiser as a result
of the experience,
and so are you.

Well — I suppose …
Yes.
Let's
do it.

So . . .

However . . .

MEN!

WOMEN!

CHAPTER TWO

PERSONAL MATTERS

PERSONAL
MATTERS

Whose fault?
ANXIETY is discovered
hiding behind **disguised jealousy --**
jealousy of whomever, or whatever
you believe is in control of,
or responsible for your unpleasant experience.
Driven by anxiety, you are likely to transfer
responsibility for your peace of mind
to a thought that will vanish
and leave you vexed.

**Problems,
like everything
else in life,
come and go.**

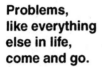

Am I the
source of the
problems
that I sometimes
have?
Why can't I
have peace
all the time?

That's when you're anxious and you wish you could.

That's a jealous notion.

A jealous notion?
What jealous notion?
Jealous of whom?

Blind jealousy actually.
Jealousy of whom
or what you feel is
responsible or in control.
It is, in fact,
an anxiety based on the
thought that you cannot
discern your destiny —
the feeling that
you are blind.

Why do friends part?
Why do some win while
others lose?
Why are there wars?
Why do people fight?

Why are you
angry now?

Your vision
of your own
helplessness,
that's
why.

Square one?

Your anxiety.

We can't be
less than personal
if we're to get
results that make sense.

Who is dissatisfied?

You.

Think about this:

**When someone
is ill or in
trouble,
and you wish
to help,
you would like
your action
to be beneficial
wouldn't you?**

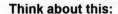

How?

**And before
you act,
don't you
decide what
to do
based on your
knowledge of
yourself
and of the
situation?**

I guess so, though I'm not always conscious of doing that. But what does that have to do with stopping anxiety?

A lot.
If you're dissatisfied, you should treat yourself as you would treat someone who's ill or in trouble — someone who you really want to help.

CHAPTER THREE

SAYING IT
AND
DOING IT

SAYING IT --
AND DOING IT

Practical Self-Management
considerations...

What are your thoughts when you hear birds or see trees?

How do you react when you hear children laugh or cry?

I've always hidden my feelings.

In the evening's fading light,
shadows were gradually lengthening,
and even though they were not far apart,
it seemed their loneliness was strengthening.

Suffering!
Always suffering!

Why do they
suffer?

**Are they
suffering?**

It is
obvious.

Well,
to be honest,
I don't know why.

I'm not sure that they're even
aware of the passion you feel
for them.

Remember, you can't control
everything that happens
to you. But your
sense of gratitude
should be at work constantly,
regardless of the situation
you're in.

If you stay conscious of that, you could often save yourself some anxiety.

73

No!
What's that supposed to mean?

That life constantly changes, and that you select your reaction to each change.

We hurt
when we do
not allow
ourselves
to accommodate to
change.

If only
doing it
were as easy
as
saying it!

CHAPTER FOUR

CHOICES

CHOICES

considerations for managing anxiety
while making positive changes

**Can you see yourself
for a moment
in terms of love?**

My tolerance is almost exhausted by love as I know it... I told you that I see love as an emotion that too often causes wrath, when inspiring peace and happiness is supposed to be its function.

Let's examine your concept of what it should be...

What does my concept
have to do with it?

**Your thoughts are
important to you...**

How
are my thoughts going
to change anything?

**Your thoughts
change you.**

So is tolerance. Quite basic and very elementary
You hurt yourself without it.

The more you know about what challenges your understanding of yourself,
the more choices you have in applying that knowledge in a constructive way to all the situations you face.

You know,
I think this conversation is elementary... very, very elementary.

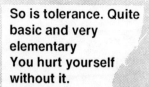

Of course, you know that all of this talk is hypothetical. It is not taking place in a situation where my patience is challenged.

Your patience will be challenged in time. It is not in the heat of fighting that a warrior trains.

Listen,
there is
a time when I
reflect
upon good
and I'm
happy —
and a time
when I
reflect upon evil
and I become sad.
And yet,
there is a time when I
remember the
good things
and I become sad,
and a time when I recall
the bad things
and I feel
strangely happy.

And I often question:
Why do I have
problems?
Is this life
one long test?
If so,
a test by what
or whose
standards?
And for what?

And then . . .?

What do you mean:
"And then"?

And then,
do you fly off
on your broom
again, with the same
unresolved
expectations?

CHAPTER FIVE

AN
INSIDE
JOB

AN
INSIDE JOB

of evaluation
and motivation

Now... what did I really expect?

You expected a joyful experience without any change at all.

Is there a right and a wrong way of dealing with expectations?

It's not really a question of right or wrong. It's more a matter of understanding that tension develops with every expectation...

...and the tension will not go away without some kind of resolution...

There comes a time to search our feelings inside out, to come to know what the joy of being is all about, and what makes that real.

Hmmmmmmm!

What now?

I must admit that I'm searching for guarantees... I'm searching for formulas to a life free from frustration.

I want to know if there's a guarantee against frustration. ..

You're not alone. There are people in history whose biographies and writings might give you new ways of looking at an old problem.

Then I shall read...

I have read to this point... Now, explain to me: Psalms 10:1 'Why standest thou afar off, O Lord? Why hidest thou thyself in times of trouble?'

What's your position?

Your position prepares your perspective. For example, do you ask out of curiosity, or do you have a sincere desire to know?

What does my position have to do with this?

99

But that was exactly what I did!

Then I decided to stop assuming that I was the last righteous, blameless person on earth...

I want to hear your story!

But here I'm actually telling you *my* story.

It seemed as though I was always in trouble of one kind or another... always frustrated for one reason or another...

And you prayed and nothing happened, right...?

Did I pray?
That's a good
question.
I know I
quarrelled and
complained and
blamed others a
lot... Did I pray?
On occasion, I
would say things
like 'Lord, help
me!'

Then what?

I discovered this
question: 'Why
standest thou
afar off, O Lord?
Why hidest thou
thyself in times
of trouble?'
And I said to myself:
"Someone wrote
my thoughts!"

What was "trouble"
for you?

The fear
I had of evil,
which was any
form of
undesirable
experience—
according to my
standards. So I
was constantly
having trouble.
I always had a
reason to be upset.

102

By what standard did you assess yourself?

By standards which I was afraid to question. So anyone who judged my standards was not good for me.

Psalms 10:1 bothered me. The idea that the Lord would hide Himself in times of trouble disturbed me. I was frightened and angry.

And then?

I began to wonder about the object of my anger, and Who was I talking to? And who was I? That was when I began to see something else in Psalms 10.

Thank you for telling me your story. However, at this point I need to know what constitutes my own story.

CHAPTER SIX

DEJA VU

DEJA VU

Life goes on
and every now and then,
you have an experience that **makes you say,
"Ah! this has happened before!"**
This chapter summarizes an
interesting new way of
looking at yourself...

YET...

He created heaven and earth... made man and woman...

and hides Himself in times of trouble...?

Hides himself in times of trouble...?

I don't understand it. But I shall no longer try to understand it. I'll just forget about it.

And I don't want to see you again, my friend.

111

That is true...

Integrity is the balancing agent for everything, through all seasons, everytime, for every purpose.

I have read in the Scriptures that 'for every thing there is a season; a time for every purpose under heaven.'*

*Eccl. 3:1

LATER... OVER REFRESHMENTS

That's Anxiety hiding behind the wall

Anxiety catches people off guard like that.

113

May I ask you
something?

Sure.

How can I develop
and maintain
integrity?

I take it you're
not asking out of
idle curiosity.

No.

Search your heart for that which you truly love, and do it as a service with all the love you can give.

Is that all?

Isn't that enough?

Hi.   Hello.

I found solutions to some
of the problems we've had
in our relationship

Good! So have I!
I also have opinions about a
friendship and they do not
include flying off on
certain expectations.

117

The answers that
I have found
can not be
expressed all
at once.

So, what do you expect
to happen now?

THE END